SMITH
Surname Study

Cincinnati, Ohio – To the Year 1840

E. S. AMONS

ii

Smith Surname Study
Cincinnati, Ohio – To the Year 1840
Copyright © 2016 E. S. Amons

iv

Index

Introduction

It is said that the city of Cincinnati was settled in 1788. That was actually the year land was bought to form a city and it began with three log cabins. Cincinnati was incorporated in 1819 as it grew.

These pages are the results of searches for every adult SMITH in Hamilton County, within the city limits of Cincinnati, Ohio up to and including the year 1840. All details found for people are listed.

Names are listed by first names. At the end of each item, the last set of numbers is the year it was found for.

At times you will see one person attached to multiple years and at other times there are multi-people of the same first name. It is up to the reader to match up what may be family members. Sometimes the occupation or home location can help match up people.

It would be great to say all early SMITH's have been found, but it is doubtful per the way records were and were not kept in the early days.

SMITH Streets

In 1819 there was a SMITH street. It ran from the Ohio River north. The first street along the Ohio River was Front and it dead-ended at Smith Street. Front, Second, Third, Fourth and Fifth crossed Smith Street.

Per 1834, Smith Street ran from the river north to 7th, west of John.

1819 Oliver Farnsworth Map

Smith Street shows in the middle of the preceding view on the left side of the houses and to the right of the open space running from the Ohio River northward.

In 1829 there is a 'Smith's Grove Alley'. It does at least connect to Seventh.

In 1829 there is a street named Smith's Grove.

...

1819 Full Oliver Farnsworth Map

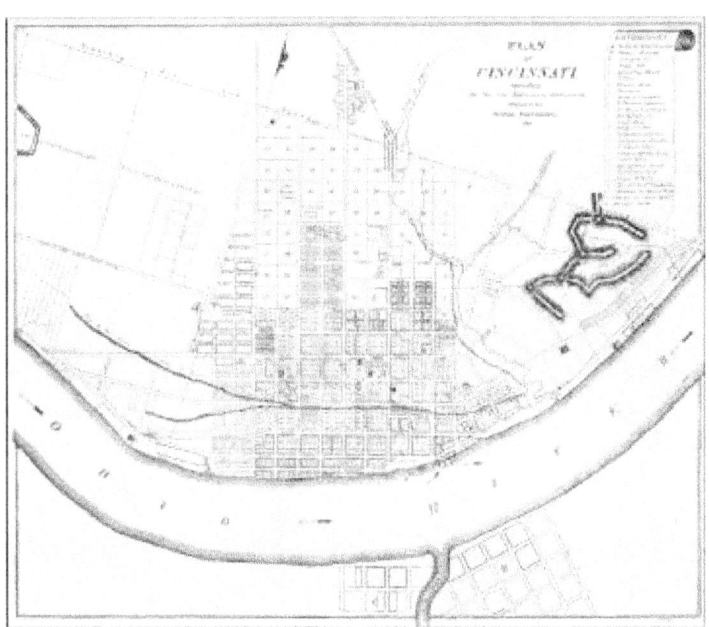

4

Businesses
Also check within the name area.

Bar and Smith, commission merchants. 5 Lower Market / Lowermarket. 1825.

Dana & Smith, grocers, Fifth between Main and Walnut. 1825.

Jess/Jesse SMITH, M.D. 1825, 1829, 1831.

Johnston SMITH & Co, merchants, 20 and 35 Main. 1825.

S. T, & SMITH Dry-goods-Merchant. N-W corner 6th and Plum. 1840.

Sanders & Smith – Drapers and Tailors. 1840.

Smith & Day Printers, 14 Main. 1836.

Smith & Jennings - Merchant-Tailors at No 107 Main street. 1840.

Smith & Foulke, innkeepers, 20 West Front. See Benjamin C. 1819.

Smith & Holabird - Engine-builders & Foundry at We Front west of Smith. 1840.

Smith & Loring, merchants, 13 Main. 1819.

Smith & McMillen, Iron and Stove Merchants at S-E corner of Main and Court. 1840.

Smith & Mason, (William Smith & Daniel Mason) iron and general commission merchants, Front between Main & Wal. 1831.

Smith & Scudder, (John R. S. & William S.) grocer, corner of Vine and North Canal. 1831.

SMITH, J. G. & Co. – Grocers. 1840.

SMITH Joseph & Co., merchants, 5 E. Front. 1829.

Smith William S. wholesale grocer and commission merchant, Green's Row, Front, home: Front between Vine & Race. 1831.

Smith Wright & Co. Wholesale grocers /and liquor store at Main near 4th. 1829, 1831.

Smyth _ _ _ & Co. merchants, Main near Front. 1829.

Truman & Smith - Booksellers, Publishers and Stationers, No. 250 Main, near Fourth Street. 1836, 1840.

SANDERS & SMITH,

DRAPERS & TAILORS,

❧205,❧

Main street, West side, between Fifth and Sixth,

Keep on hand a good assortment of CLOTHS, CASSIMERES, and VESTINGS, which they are prepared to make up at the shortest notice, and upon reasonable terms.

1839 Sanders & Smith

Inhabitant Totals

The 'inhabitant' totals stated from 1795 for the years up to and including 1835, as published in 1836 follow:

1795 = 500

1800 = 750

1805 = 960

1810 = 2320

1813 = 4000

1819 = 10,283

1824 = 12,016

1826 = 16,230

1829 = 24,148

In 1829 it is stated "From the most correct data that we have been able to obtain, there are at present, a permanent white population in Cincinnati, consisting of Males – 11,855; Females – 10,035, totaling white inhabitants at 21,890; to which may be added blacks and mulattoes 2,258. The total being 24,148 souls."

1833 = 27,645

1835 = 29,000

No First Name

_____ SMITH – Works as a laborer. Boards at Rachael Sloan's who has no listing. 1831.

_____ SMITH – He/She was a laborer. He/She worked &/or lived on Court between Elm and Plumb. 1834.

_____ SMITH – He/She was a morocco dresser and boarded at S. L. Marchant's. Marchant worked or owned Swan Tavern and is found on 9th between Main and Sycamore. 1834.

_____ Mrs. SMITH – Officer, 2nd Directress, Female Infant School Society. "Recently organized – The design of this highly laudable institution is to impart instruction to male and female children under the age of six years. To obtain admittance into the school it is required that the child be free from any contagious disorder, and shall have passed regularly through the vaccine disease, or shall submit to immediate vaccination." 1829.

_____ Mrs. SMITH – She is found on 5th between Sycamore and Broadway. 1834.

_____ Mrs. SMITH – She was a seamstress. She lived &/or worked on Elm between Front and 2d. 1836.

A First Names

Abigail Mrs. SMITH – She is found on George between Race and Elm. 1834.

Abraham SMITH – Ward 4, Cincinnati. 1820.

Abraham SMITH – Birth 1761. Death 1824. Fought in the American Revolution. Nativity: New Jersey.

Abraham SMITH – He is listed on the 1810 Hamilton County tax list. In 1819 he was a laborer. He worked &/or lived at the north corner of Elm and Water. 1819.

Adam SMITH – Worked at a coffee house. He worked &/or lived on 5th between Main and Walnut. 1834.

Adam SMITH – He was a glue maker. He boarded at Mrs. M. Betts. This may be Martha Betts who is a widow found on 'Western Row north Cor. Line'. 1834.

Adam SMITH – He had a boarding house at 'W s Race between 5th and 6th.' 1836.

Adam SMITH – Ward 5, Cincinnati. 1840.

Alban G. SMITH – He was a physician. He worked &/or lived on Walnut between 3d and 4th. 1834.
Alban G. SMITH – He was a physician with his office on Vine near 5th. He boarded at Mrs. Susan Turner's boarding house at 'S s 5th between Sycamore and Broadway'. 1836.

Albert P. SMITH - Woodward College, Rooms on Harrison St., Nativity: Virginia. 1840.

Alfred SMITH – Ward 3, Cincinnati. 1840.

Alfred D. SMITH – He was a pump and block maker. He worked &/or lived on Front between Ludlow and Lawrence. 1834.

Alfred D. SMITH – He was a pump and block maker. He lived &/or worked on Front between Ludlow and Lawrence. 1836.

Alpheus SMITH – He was a carpenter. He worked &/or lived on Fifth between Plum and Western Row. His nativity was New York. 1825.

Alpheus SMITH – He is a carpenter. He worked &/or lived on 4th between Elm and Plumb. 1829.

Alpheus SMITH – Ward 2, Cincinnati. 1830.

Alpheus SMITH – He was a carpenter. He worked &/or lived on 4th between Elm and Plumb. 1831.

Alpheus SMITH – He was a carpenter. He worked &/or lived on Western Row north of Chestnut. 1834.

Alpheus SMITH – He was a carpenter. He lived &/or worked on John between Laurel and Hopkins. 1836.

Alpheus SMITH – Carpenter. resided on John between Laurel and Hopkins. Nativity N.J. 1840.

Alpheus SMITH – Ward 7, Cincinnati. 1840.

Alpheus SMITH – Birth: 23 Feb 1796. Death: 1 Aug 1859, Paralysis. Parents: Alex. & Elizth. Funeral director: J. P. Epply. Burial: Spring Grove, Sec 39, Lot 108.

Amasa SMITH – Ward 6, Cincinnati. 1840.

Andrew SMITH – He was a laborer. He worked &/or lived on Western Row between Sixth and Seventh. His nativity was Tennessee. 1825.

Andrew K. SMITH – Sycamore Township. Age 26-45, wife age 26-45, son 1 up to age 10, daughters 2 up to age 10. Occupation: Agriculture. 1820.

Ann Mrs. SMITH – She was found on 6th near Smith. 1836.

Ann Mrs. SMITH – She was found on 7th between Main and Walnut. 1836.

Augustus SMITH – Ward 4, Cincinnati. 1830.
Augustine SMITH – He was a brick layer. He worked &/or lives on Front near Pike. 1831.
Augustus SMITH – He was a mason. He worked &/or lived on Longworth between Plumb and Western row. 1834.
Augustine SMITH – He was a mason. He lived &/or worked on 'N s 6th near John'. 1836.
Augustus SMITH - Brick-layer. Home: Mercer near Vine. Nativity: Virginia. 1840.

B First Names

B. SMITH – Ward 4, Cincinnati. 1830.

B. SMITH – He was a painter. He worked &/or lived on Front between Vine and Race. 1834.

B. B. SMITH – He was a carpenter. He worked &/or lived on 6th between John and Smith. 1834.

B. C. SMITH – He was a bar keeper. He is found at 'Commercial Exchange'. 1834.

B. C. SMITH – Ward 5, Cincinnati. 1840.

B. W. SMITH – Ward 7, Cincinnati. 1840.

Ballard SMITH – Birth, date unknown. Death 1794. Nativity: Virginia.

Barney SMITH – Ward 1, Cincinnati. 1840.

Belts SMITH – Male, White, Widower, age 74 years, died 2 Feb 1881 from 'Chr. Rheumatism'. He lived &/or died at 28 Hopkins St. The funeral director was Epply. Cemetery: Spring Grove.

Benjamin SMITH – Ward 4, Cincinnati. 1820.

Benjamin SMITH – Ward 5, Cincinnati. 1830.

Benjamin SMITH – Ward 2, Cincinnati. 1840.

Benjamin SMITH – He was a constable. He worked &/or lived on Front between Vine and Race. 1834.

Benjamin SMITH – He worked as a shoemaker. He worked &/or lived at 85 West Front. 1819.
Benjamin SMITH – He worked as a shoemaker. He worked &/or lived on Vine between Front and Second. His nativity was New York. 1825.
Benjamin SMITH – He was a shoemaker. He worked &/or lived on 7th between John and Mound. 1829.
Benjamin SMITH – He was a shoemaker. He worked &/or lived on Water between Race and Elm. 1831.
Benjamin SMITH - Shoe-maker. Home: Lodges Street. Nativity: N.Y. 1840.

Benjamin SMITH – He was a tailor. He worked &/or lived on Broadway between 6th & 7th. 1831.

Benjamin SMITH – He was a carpenter. He worked &/or lived on Elizabeth west of Western Row. 1829.

Benjamin SMITH – No occupation listed. He lived &/or worked on 2d between Elm and Plum. 1836.

Benjamin C. SMITH – Worked as an innkeeper. He worked &/or lived at 20 West Front. 1819.

Benjamin C. SMITH – He is listed as a carter. He worked &/or lived on Race near Northern Row. 1831.

Benjamin E. SMITH – He was a grocer. He worked &/or lived on the corner of 6th and plumb. 1829.

Benjamin. F. SMITH - Clerk at B. Sterrett's dry-goods merchant at 8 Lower Market. Nativity: N.Y. 1840.

Bernard J. SMITH – He was a clerk and boarded at the Broadway Hotel. 1834.

Benjamin R. SMITH – Ward 5, Cincinnati. 1830.
Benjamin R. SMITH – He was a house carpenter. He worked &/or lived on 6th near John. 1831.
Benjamin R. SMITH – Carpenter. Home: 6th between John and Smith Streets. Nativity: R.I. 1840.
Benjamin R. SMITH – Ward 7, Cincinnati. 1840.

Benjamin Y. SMITH (Gregory & Smith) printer. Business at Main by Front and 2d. He boards at Mrs. M. Smith's. 1834.
Benjamin Y. SMITH – He worked at or owned Smith & Day printer at 14 Main. Home: Longworth between Plum and Western Row. 1836.

Biten SMITH – Ward 4, Cincinnati. 1830.

Blackstone S. SMITH – He is found on 7th between Western and John. 1831.

Briggs SMITH – He worked at or owned a coffeehouse. He worked &/or lived at 8 Johnston's Row. 1831
Briggs SMITH – No occupation listed. He is found on 5th between Western Row and John. 1834.

Briggs SMITH – He was a clerk at the Erastus Poor grocery located at 'S s 5th between Main and Walnut'. 1836.

Briggs SMITH - Home: Appears he rents from E. Poor & Co, wholesale and retail grocer, at their shop location at 5th between Main and Walnut. Nativity N.Y. 1840.

Briton E. SMITH – He was a painter. He worked &/or lived on Race between 2d and Front. 1829.

Burres SMITH – Ward 1, Cincinnati. 1820.

Burrows W. SMITH – Cabinet maker at Barton White's cabinet maker shop. Boards on 3d between Wood and Mill streets. Nativity: Ohio. 1840.

C First Names

C. SMITH — Secretary, the Weslyan [Wesleyan] Sunday School Society. 1829.

Calvin SMITH — He was a clerk and boarded at the John Elstner [Elster] boarding house at the corner of Broadway and 6th. 1834.

Charles SMITH — There is a Charles on the 1810 Hamilton County tax list.

Charles SMITH — Worked as an innkeeper. He worked &/or lived at 3 corner Main and Water. 1819.

Charles SMITH — Ward 4, Cincinnati. 1820.

Charles SMITH — He worked at or owned a boarding house. He worked &/or lived on Front between Main and Sycamore. His nativity was Pennsylvania. 1825.

Charles SMITH — He was a hatter. He worked &/or lived on 3d between Main and Walnut. 1829.

Charles SMITH — He was a clerk at Jas Irwin [not listed]. He boards at the Main St. Hotel. 1834.

Charles SMITH — He was a cabinet maker. He lived &/or worked on 8th between Western Row and John. 1836.

Charles SMITH — Cabinet-maker at William Morehouse's located at 18 1/2 East 4th. Home: N s 6th between Elm and Plum. Nativity: Pennsylvania. 1840.

Charles SMITH — He was a tobacconist. He worked &/or lived on Plumb between 9th and Court. 1834.
Charles SMITH — He was a tobacconist. He lived &/or worked at the southeast corner of Walnut and Plum. 1836.

Charles SMITH [#1] — Ward 1, Cincinnati. 1840.

Charles SMITH [#2] — Ward 2, Cincinnati. 1840.

Charles SMITH [#3] — Ward 4, Cincinnati. 1840.

Charles SMITH [#4] — Ward 7, Cincinnati. 1840.

Charles SMITH — Resides at the alley at the Elbow of the Canal. Nativity: N.Y. 1840.

Charles SMITH - Book-binder. Lives at George W. Tuxworth's also a book-binder. Both appear to work at Josiah Drake's, book-seller and stationer at No 14 Main. Nativity: Both Smith and Tuxworth are from Maryland. 1840.

Charles J. SMITH — He worked at or owned a wholesale grocery and produce store at 'N s 5th near Vine. Home: Longworth near Plum. 1836.

Charles J. W. SMITH - Confectioner, W s Main 4 doors N of 9. Nativity: Pennsylvania. 1840.

Charles P. SMITH – Ward 2, Cincinnati. 1820.

Charles. P. SMITH – He was a hatter. He worked &/or lived on the corner of Longworth and Elm. 1834.

Charles W. SMITH - Clerk at Smith & McMillan's iron and stove merchants. Nativity: N.Y. 1840.

Chloe SMITH – Ward 5, Cincinnati. 1840.

Christopher SMITH – Ward 1, Cincinnati. 1830.

Christopher SMITH – Ward 1, Cincinnati. 1840.

Christopher SMITH – Worked as a cabinet maker at 98 Sycamore. Home: 100 Sycamore. 1819.

Christopher SMITH – He was a cabinet maker. He worked &/or lived on Sycamore between Fourth and Fifth. His nativity was England. 1825.

Christopher SMITH. He was a cabinet maker. He worked &/or lived on Sycamore between 4th and 5th. [See William B.] 1829.

Christopher, SMITH – He worked as a cabinetmaker. He worked &/or lived on Sycamore between 4th and 5th. 1831.

Christopher SMITH – He was a cabinet maker. He worked &/or lived on Sycamore between 4th and 5th. 1834.

Christopher SMITH – He was a cabinet maker. He lived &/or worked on 'E s Sycamore between 4th and 5th'. 1836.

Christopher SMITH - Cabinet maker and Undertaker, E s Sycamore between 4th and 5th. Nativity: England. 1840.

Clara SMITH – Ward 1, Cincinnati. 1840.

Clarrisa SMITH [#1] – Ward 5, Cincinnati. 1840.

Clarrisa SMITH [#2] – Ward 7, Cincinnati. 1840.

Conrad SMITH – He was a silversmith. He boarded at Mrs. Tomlinson's (Mrs. Clarinda Tomlinson, boarding house, Sycamore north of 4th). 1829.
Conrad SMITH - Silver-smith and Jeweler. Boarded on 4th near Sycamore. Nativity: Pennsylvania. 1840.

Constantine SMITH – There is a Constantine on the 1810 Hamilton County tax list.

Crammon SMITH – He was a blacksmith and boarded at the A. Lucas boarding house on Sycamore between 2d and Lower Market. 1834.

D First Names

Daniel SMITH – Ward 4, Cincinnati. 1820.

Daniel SMITH – He was a clerk at Mirick Smith's grocery. 1831.

Daniel SMITH – He worked at or owned a coffee house. He worked &/or lived at the corner of Race and 2d. 1834.

Daniel SMITH – Owns &/or works at Stillman & Smith coal dealers. Resides on Race between 3d and Pearl. Nativity: Vermont. 1840.

Daniel SMITH – Carpenter. Boards at George Palmer's. Nativity: Vermont. 1840.

Daniel SMITH – Ward 4, Cincinnati. 1840.

David SMITH – He was an engineer. He lived &/or worked at the junction of Front and Water. 1836.

David SMITH [#1] – Ward 6, Cincinnati. 1840.

David SMITH [#2] – Ward7, Cincinnati. 1840.

David J. SMITH – Works at or owns Smith & Holabird. Home: West Front west of Smith. Nativity: N.Y. 1840.

David H. SMITH – He was a teamster. He lived &/or worked on Canal between Elm and Plum. 1836.

E First Names

E. SMITH – He was a clerk at Charles Fisher's wholesale grocery on Main between 2d and Pearl. He boards at Cyrus Coffin's boarding house on Main between 3d and 4th. 1834.

E. B. Mrs. SMITH – Vice President of the Female Branch Bible Society. 1829.

E. C. SMITH – Works as a Director for the Commercial Bank at No. 45, Main Street. This bank was incorporate in the winter of 1829 but was not organized until April, 1831, and is now [1831] doing business. 1831.

Ebenezer SMITH – Carpenter at the 'Planing Machine', East Front near the Rolling Mill. 1840.

Edmund SMITH – Ward 3, Cincinnati. 1820.

Edmund C. SMITH – He was a merchant. He worked &/or lived at 20 Main. His nativity was Connecticut. 1825.
Edmund C. SMITH - He worked &/or lived on 5th between Sycamore and Broadway. 1831.
Edmund C. SMITH – He was a produce Merchant. He worked &/or lived on Front near Walnut. He is listed as a city officer being on the City Council in the 1st Ward. 1831.

Edward SMITH – There is an Edward on the 1810 Hamilton County tax list.

Edward SMITH – He worked as a merchant. Home was at 251 Main. 1819.

Edward SMITH – He worked as a turner and whitesmith. He worked &/or lived on Sycamore between Third and Fourth. His nativity was Massachusetts. 1825.

Edward SMITH – He was a laborer. He boarded at Abbott Goddard's. Abbott was a merchant who lived or worked on 5th between Vine and Race. 1831.

Edward C. SMITH – Ward 1, Cincinnati. 1830.

Edward C. SMITH – (Johnston, Smith & Co.) He worked &/or lived on Main at 2d. 1829.

Edward G. SMITH – He was a pump maker. He worked &/or lived on Front north of Ludlow. 1829.
Edward G. SMITH – He is a pump and block maker working at Front between Ludlow and Lawrence. Home: Pike near Lawrence. 1831.
Edward SMITH – He was a block and pump maker. He worked &/or lived on Front between Elm and Plumb. 1834.

Edwin SMITH – He works as a Clerk. Home: Walnut between Columbia and Front. Nativity: N.J. 1840.

Elijah SMITH – He worked at or owned Doyle & Smith and was a merchant tailor. He lived &/or worked on Green between Race and Elm. 1836.

Elijah SMITH – Works at or owns Smith & Jennings. Home: 3d between Walnut and Vine. Nativity: Virginia. 1840.

Eliza Mrs. SMITH – Home: Corner of Vine and 7th, Nativity: N.Y. 1840.

Elizabeth SMITH – resides Sycamore between Sixth and Seventh streets. Her nativity was New Jersey. 1825.

Elizabeth SMITH – Ward 1, Cincinnati. 1830.

Elizabeth SMITH – She is found at the corner of John and Catharine. 1834.

Elizabeth SMITH – She was a mantua maker. She worked &/or lived near the corner of Sycamore and Lower Market. 1831.
Elizabeth Mrs. SMITH – She is found at the corner of Sycamore and Lower Market. 1834.
Elizabeth SMITH – She was a mantua maker. He lived &/or worked on sycamore near Lower Market. 1836.
Elizabeth Mrs. SMITH - Mantua-maker. Home: Southwest corner of Sycamore and Lower Market. Nativity: Maryland. 1840.

Elizabeth Mrs. SMITH – She is listed as near the corner of 6th & Sycamore. 1831.
Elizabeth Mrs. SMITH – She is found on 6th between Sycamore and Broadway. 1834.

Elizabeth Mrs. SMITH – She boarded at Mrs. Ann Miller's on Lodge's Alley between 5th and 6th. 1836.

Elizabeth Mrs. SMITH – She was found on 3d between Western Row and John. 1836.

Elizabeth Mrs. SMITH – Seamstress. Home: Between 4th and 5th and John and Smith streets. Nativity: Maryland. 1840.

Elias SMITH – No profession shown. Lives or works at 6th between Smith and Mound. 1829.

Elijah SMITH – He was a tailor at 3d north of Main. Home: Green between Elm and Plumb. 1834.

Elijah SMITH – Ward 4, Cincinnati. 1840.

Elmarion SMITH – He was a brick maker. He worked &/or lived on Longworth north of Smith. 1829.

Emily SMITH – Born 1820.

Emrick SMITH – No occupation listed. He boards at D. Smiths who has no listing this year. 1834.

Esther SMITH – Born 1746.

F First Names

Fanny SMITH – Ward 1, Cincinnati. 1840.

Fielding B. SMITH – Ward 5, Cincinnati. 1830.

Fielding C. SMITH - River Trader. Home: Race between Front and Columbia streets. Nativity: Virginia. 1840.

Francis SMITH – Ward 6, Cincinnati. 1840.

Francis SMITH – It only says "at John Jolley's." Information for John Jolly is: Secretary Cincinnati Equitable Insurance Comp. Home 6th between John and Smith. Office 4th near Main. 1831.

Francis SMITH – (col'd). She was found at the southwest corner of 6th & Vine. 1836.

Francis C. SMITH - Clerk at J. H. Warner & Co's. Boards at Franklin House. Nativity: Connecticut. 1840.

Francis Mrs. SMITH – She was a bandbox manufacturer. He lived &/or worked on Plum between Front and 2d. 1836.

Frances Mrs. SMITH - Boards N s 5th near the Mound. Nativity: N.J. 1840.

Frank SMITH – Ward 2, Cincinnati. 1820.

Frank SMITH – He was a laborer. He worked &/or lived at the corner of Vine and 6th. 1831.

Frederic SMITH – Ward 7, Cincinnati. 1840.

Frederick SMITH - Carpenter and Joiner. Home: S s Canal near Vine. Nativity: German. 1840.

Frederick SMITH – Plasterer. Home: Race near 13th. Nativity: Pennsylvania. 1840.

Frederick SMITH - Shoe-maker. Boarded at Chas Lawler's, also a shoe-maker. Nativity: Pennsylvania. 1840.

G First Names

G. G. SMITH – He works for the fire department on Engine No. 1 as 'assistant' under the Foreman John Tatem. The Engine has '52 members'. 1831.

G. W. SMITH – He was a carpenter. He boards at Edward Dodson's who is also a carpenter and is shown at the corner of Walnut and 6th. 1834.

Gannus SMITH – Ward 4, Cincinnati. 1840.

George SMITH – There is a mention in an obit on 8 April 1828 in the Cincinnati Daily Gazette. The obit may be for a family member.

George SMITH – President Judge of Common Pleas, 6th Circuit. 1829.

George SMITH – He worked as a saddletree maker on 6th near Western Row. Home: Road to Mill Creek. 1831.

George SMITH – He was a blacksmith. He worked &/or lived on main between Canal and 12th. 1831

George Capt. SMITH – He boards at Cincinnati Hotel. 1831.

George SMITH – He was a shoe maker. He worked &/or lived on Sycamore between 3d and 4th. 1834.

George SMITH [#1] – Ward 1, Cincinnati. 1840.

George SMITH [#2] – Ward 1, Cincinnati. 1840.

George SMITH – Male, White, Single, age 69 years, died 19 Jul 1884 from Colitis. He lived &/or died at 169 Barr St. Funeral director: Mulvihill. Cemetery: Spring Grove. Nativity: Ireland.

George A. SMITH – Grocer. Lived &/or worked at the Northwest corner of Elm and 5th. Nativity: N.Y. 1840.

George G. SMITH – He was a grocer. He worked &/or lived on the corner of Front and Vine. 1829.
George G. SMITH – He was a grocer. He worked &/or lived at the corner of Front and Vine. 1831.
George SMITH – He was a grocer on East Front. Home: Race between 3d and 4th. 1834.
George E. SMITH – He was a grocer. He worked &/or lived on the corner of Front and Vine. 1834. [The middle initial may be a misprint or he is a son. Note the Front St location.]
George G. SMITH – He was a grocer. He lived &/or worked at the northeast corner of Front & Vine. 1836. [Note the Front St. location.]
George SMITH – He was a commission and produce merchant at 'E s Broadway near Front. Home: 6th near the Medical College. 1836.
George G. SMITH – Ward 4, Cincinnati. 1840.

George H. SMITH – He was a carpenter. He worked &/or lived on Front between Western Row and Mill. 1829.

George Hitchner SMITH – Listed as a first family.

George P. SMITH – Ward 4, Cincinnati. 1830.

George R. SMITH - Deputy Clerk Superior Court. Home: Southwest corner Court and Elm. Nativity: England. 1840.

George R. SMITH – Ward 5, Cincinnati. 1840.

George W. SMITH – He was a Street Commissioner in the Fourth Ward. 1836.
George SMITH - Street Commissioner 4th district. Home: corner of Front and Vine. Nativity: Massachusetts. 1840.

George W. SMITH – He was a carpenter. He boarded at Edward Dodson's at the corner of Sixth and Walnut. 1829.
George W. SMITH – He was a carpenter. He boards at Edward Dodson's at the corner of Walnut and 6th. 1831.
George SMITH – He was a carpenter and boarded at Edward Dodson's at the northwest corner of 6th & Walnut. 1836.
George SMITH – Carpenter. Boarded at Edward Dodson's at 'N s 6th near Walnut'. Nativity: N.J. 1840.

Gillian M. SMITH – Listed as a first family. No details.

Green H. SMITH – He was a carpenter. He worked &/or lived on Front between Western Row and Mill. 1829.
G. H. SMITH – He was a carpenter. He worked &/or lived on Plumb between Front and 2d. 1831.

Greg SMITH – He was a signer to a petition to Congress, signed on 13 July 1799. It had to do with land purchased.

H First Names

H. SMITH – Ward 5, Cincinnati. 1830.

H. SMITH – He was working as a carpet weaver. He worked &/or lived on Elm near Northern Row. 1831.

Hannah SMITH – Ward 1, Cincinnati. 1840.

Hannah Jane SMITH – Born 1771. Died 1859. Nativity: NJ.

Hannah SMITH – Born 1808. Died 1888. Nativity: Ohio.

Harry SMITH – He was a millwright. He worked &/or lived on Front near Deer Creek. 1829.
Harry SMITH – He worked as a millwright. He worked &/or lived on Front near Deer Creek bridge. 1831.

Harry SMITH – He was a ship carpenter. He lived &/or worked on east Front near the Deer Creek bridge. 1836. [See Henry.]

Henry SMITH – He was a laborer. He worked &/or lived at the north-west junction of Front and Fifth. 1819.

Henry SMITH – Ward 2, Cincinnati. 1820.

Henry SMITH – Ward 3, Cincinnati. 1830.

Henry SMITH [#1] – Ward 5, Cincinnati. 1830.

Henry SMITH [#2] – Ward 5, Cincinnati. 1830.

Henry SMITH – Ward 6, Cincinnati. 1840.

Henry SMITH – He worked as a carpenter. He was a boarder at A.G. Hamlin's. [This may be an error and is Hannibal G. Hamlin who was a carpenter. Hannibal G. is listed at the corner of Pike & Symmes.] 1831.

Henry SMITH – He was a laborer. He worked &/or lived on Woodward between Sycamore & Broadway. 1834.

Henry SMITH – He was a bricklayer. He boarded at J. Miller's. This may be Jacob Miller who was also a bricklayer. The home was on 5th between Mill and Wood. 1829.

Henry SMITH – He was a clerk at Donaldson's. He boards at Dennison's. 1831.

Henry SMITH – He was an engineer. He lived &/or worked at the junction of Front and Water. 1836.

Henry SMITH - Machinist, 'in' Friendship St. Home: Broadway between Columbia and Congress. Nativity: N.Y. 1840.

Henry SMITH – He was a ship carpenter. He lived &/or worked on east Front near the corp. line. 1836. (See Harry.) Henry SMITH - Ship Carpenter. Home: E Front near the Corporation line. Nativity: Ohio. 1840.

Henry J. SMITH – He was a laborer. He worked &/or lived at the corner of Broadway and Court. 1829.

Henry M. SMITH - Finisher at Smith & Holabird's engine builders and foundry. Home: Front St. west of Smith St. Nativity: N.Y. 1840.

Henry R. SMITH – He was a cabinet maker. He worked &/or lived on seventh between Main and Walnut. His nativity was England. 1825.

Henry R. SMITH – Pork Merchant at the corner of Court and Sycamore. Boarded at the Southwest corner of Elm and Court. Nativity: Kentucky. 1840.
Henry R. SMITH – Ward 5, Cincinnati. 1840.

Hezekiah SMITH – He worked as a drayman. He worked &/or lived at the corner of Plum and Water. 1819.
Hezekiah SMITH – Ward 4, Cincinnati. 1820.
Hezekiah born 1714. [This must be the father.]

Hugh SMITH – Laborer at Groesbeck's Pork-house. Nativity: Scottish. 1840.

Hugh SMITH – Brick layer. Boarded at Roger's in Cherry Alley. Nativity: Ohio. 1840.

Hugh H. SMITH – He worked as a shoemaker. He boarded at Robert Smith's. 1829.
Hugh SMITH – He was a shoemaker. He worked &/or lived on 5th between Main and Walnut. 1831.

I First Names

Isaac SMITH – There is an Isaac on the 1810 Hamilton County tax list.

Isaac SMITH – He was a laborer. He lived &/or worked on east Front near Newell's tan yard. 1836.

Isaac SMITH – Ward 1, Cincinnati. 1840.

J First Names

J. SMITH – He was a Director of the Cincinnati Life Insurance Company. The office was on Front between Main and Sycamore streets. 1831.

J. G. SMITH & Co - Grocers & Com-Merchants at the northwest corner of Walnut & 5th. 1840.

J. G. SMITH - [Owns J. G. Smith & Co.] Home: N s 6th between Walnut and Vine. Nativity: Scottish. 1840.

J. M. SMITH – Occupation: Follows River. Home: Front between Elm and Plum. Nativity: Kentucky. 1840.

Jackson SMITH – Grocer at the corner at Wharf & Cassilly's Row. Home: Broadway between Columbia and Congress. Nativity: Virginia. 1840.

Jacob SMITH – Ward 1, Cincinnati. 1830.

Jacob SMITH [#1] – Ward 1, Cincinnati. 1840.

Jacob SMITH [#2] – Ward 3, Cincinnati. 1840.

Jacob SMITH – He was a cooper and worked at Richard Lawrence's. Richard is shown as a cooper who lived &/or worked at Vine between Front and 2d. 1836.

Jacob SMITH – He worked at or owned a coffee shop. He lived &/or worked at the southwest corner of 2d and Plum. 1836.

James SMITH – There is a James SMITH shown on the 1802 map of Cincinnati. He is on the right in the first row, marked #4. [See 1802 map.]

James SMITH – He was a pilot [ship pilot]. He worked &/or lived on Gano between Walnut and Vine. 1834.

Jacob SMITH – No occupation shown. He worked &/or lived above Canal between Vine and Race. 1829.

Jacob SMITH – He was a drayman and boarded at G. T. Marsh's. 1831.

Jacob SMITH – He was a cook. He worked &/or lived on 8th between Broadway and Sycamore. 1831.

Jacob SMITH – He was a butcher. He boarded at Henry Tesh's, who was a butcher. It appears he lived or worked on Vine between 12th and Canal. 1831.

Jacob SMITH – Male, White, Single. Death 21 Sep 1866 age 65 years at 'Comml.' Hospital from Pneumonia. Nativity German.

James SMITH – Born, 1763. Died, 1834. Nativity: PA.
James SMITH – There is a James who was the Sheriff in 1792.

James Trabue, Rev. SMITH – Born 1757. Died 1800. Nativity: Virginia.

James SMITH – President, the Mutual Relief Society of Journeymen Hatters, Instituted in 1819. 1819.

James SMITH – He worked as a moulder. He worked &/or lived on Longworth between Smith and Mound. 1819.

James SMITH – Ward 4, Cincinnati. 1820.

James SMITH – He worked as a hatter. Home was on West Second between Main and Walnut. 1819.
James SMITH – He was a hatter. He worked &/or lived on Sycamore between Second and Lower Market. His nativity was Pennsylvania. 1825.

James SMITH – He was a steam boat pilot. He worked &/or lived at Main above St. Clair. His nativity was New Jersey. 1825.
James SMITH – He was a pilot [steam boat pilot]. He worked &/or lived at alley between 6th and 7th. 1829.
James B. SMITH – He was a pilot [steamship]. He worked &/or lived on Gano between Vine and Walnut. 1831.

James SMITH – Ward 5, Cincinnati.

James SMITH – Ward 6, Cincinnati. 1840.

James SMITH – He was a pilot on the river and boarded at Mrs. E. F. Bisel's boarding house on George between Race & Elm. 1836.

James SMITH – He was a saddler. He worked &/or lived on Walnut between Third and Fourth. His nativity was Rhode Island. 1825.

James SMITH – He was a saddler. He worked &/or lived on George between Race and Elm. 1831.

James SMITH – He was a shoe maker. He worked &/or lived at Augustine Smith's. 1831.

James SMITH – This says only 'New' which may be the name of the street. 1829.

James SMITH – He worked as a river trader. He worked &/or lived on Front between Western Row and Mill. 1829.

James SMITH - Clerk at H. R. Smith's. Nativity: English. 1840.

James SMITH - Machinist 'in' Friendship St. Home: Broadway between Columbia and Congress. Nativity: English. 1840.

James SMITH - Clerk at Isherwood's stove manufacturer at 88 Main. Home: 3d between Western Row & John. Nativity: English. 1840.

James SMITH – Coal carter at James Hobson's coal merchant. Nativity: English. 1840.

James SMITH – Male, White, Married, age 53 death 30 Apr 1871 from Pneumonia at Cincinnati Hospital. Funeral director: Jones. Nativity: Virginia.

James SMITH – Male, White, Married, age 62, died 7 Jul 1878 from chronic diarrhea, liver and heart disease. He lived &/or died at 110 Butler St. His doctor was the coroner, Dr. Stich. Funeral director: Sullivan. Cemetery: St. Joseph's New. Occupation: Carpenter. Nativity: Ireland.

James SMITH – Male, White, Married, age 68, died 20 Jan 1884 from Chr. Nephritis'. He lived &/or died at 207 Everett St. Funeral director: Sullivan. Cemetery: Spring Grove. Nativity: Ireland.

James R. SMITH - Clerk at J. G. Smith & Co's. Nativity: Scottish. 1840.

James S. SMITH – Ward 7, Cincinnati. 1840.

James S. SMITH – He was a wagon maker. He worked &/or lived on 8th between Race and Elm. 1829.
James S. SMITH – He was a wagon maker. He lived &/or worked on 'W s Sycamore between Abigail and Woodward'. 1836.

James S. SMITH - Truss Hoop maker. Home: Woodward between Main & Sycamore. Nativity: Pennsylvania. 1840.

James W. SMITH - Clerk at Canal Foundry. Home: S s 3d between Western Row and John. Nativity: England. 1840.

Jane SMITH – Ward 3, Cincinnati. 1830.

Jane Ann SMITH – born 1825.

Jane Ann SMITH – Female, White, Widow, age 97 years [estimated birth 1789], died 28 Mar 1886 from General Debility. She lived &/or died at 45 Observatory Rd. Funeral director: Mulvihill. Cemetery: St. Joseph Old. Nativity: Virginia.

Jane M. SMITH – Female, White, Widow, age 97, died Jun 12 1886 from an accidental fall – concussion of brain, She lived &/or died at St. James Place. Funeral director: Estep. Cemetery: Spring Grove. Nativity: Ireland. Another report gives the 'event date' as 6 Dec 1886 and mothers name KEATING.

Jenet [Janet ?] SMITH – Ward 3, Cincinnati. 1820.
Jeremiah SMITH – There is a Jeremiah on the 1810 Hamilton County tax list.

Jeremiah SMITH – He was a whitewasher. He worked &/or lived at the rear on Elm between Front and 2d. 1831.

.

Jesse SMITH, M.D. - He worked &/or lived on Walnut between Third and Fourth. His nativity was New Hampshire. 1825.
Jesse SMITH, M.D. - Professor of Anatomy and Surgery, Medical College of Ohio. 1825.
Lunatick [Lunatic] Asylum of Ohio: A brick building, constructed and well finished by Dr. Smith, expressly as a lecture room, for all the branches except Chemistry, is provided entirely at the expense of the professors, whose

courses are conducted in it, with their own apparatus and cabinets. 1825.

Jesse SMITH, Dr. – 1st Vice President of the Humane Society, founded 1819 for the purpose of resuscitating drowned persons. Apparatus have been provided for the purpose, and proper houses built to deposit them in. 1825.

Jesse SMITH – Vice President of "The First District Medial Society of Ohio". 1825.

Jesse SMITH – He was a physician & surgeon. He worked &/or lived on Walnut between 3d and 4th. 1829.

Jesse SMITH – Professor of Surgery in Ohio Medical College. He is listed also as 'Physician – Member of the Medical Society'. He worked &/or lived on Race between 3d and 4th. 1831.

.

Jesse SMITH – Age 26-45, wife 26-45, son 1 up to age 10. Occupation: Manufacturing. 1820.

Jesse SMITH – He was a millwright. He worked &/or lived on Fourth between Race and Elm. His nativity was New York. 1825.

Jesse SMITH – He was a millwright. He worked &/or lived on Front between Western Row and Mill. 1829.

Jesse SMITH [#1] – Ward 2, Cincinnati. 1830.

Jesse SMITH [#2] – Ward 4, Cincinnati. 1830.

Jesse SMITH – He boards at Isaiah Wing's who is not listed. 1831.

Jesse SMITH – He was an engineer. He worked &/or lived on Front between Mill and Western Row. 1831.

Jesse SMITH – "Engine Factory, south side Front between John and Smith, owned by Jesse Smith, works driven by steam power." 1836.

Jesse SMITH – He worked at or owned a finishing shop. He lived &/or worked at the junction of Front and Water. 1836.

Jesse Mrs. SMITH – She is found on Walnut between 3d and 4th. 1834.

Jesse N. SMITH – Sycamore Township. Age 26-45, wife 26-45, son 1 up to age 10. Occupation: Manufacturing. 1820.

Jonathan SMITH – There is a Jonathan on the 1810 Hamilton County tax list.

John SMITH [#1] – Ward 2, Cincinnati. 1820.
John SMITH [#2] – Ward 2, Cincinnati. 1820.

John SMITH – There is a John on the 1810 Hamilton County tax list.

John SMITH - Treasurer of First Female Society of Cincinnati for Charitable and Religious Purposes. 1819.

John SMITH – Worked as a merchant. Home: Sixth Street between Walnut and Vine. 1819.

John SMITH [#1] – Ward 4, Cincinnati. 1820.

John SMITH [#2] – Ward 4, Cincinnati. 1820.

John SMITH [#1] – Ward 1, Cincinnati. 1830.

John SMITH [#2] – Ward 2, Cincinnati. 1830.

John SMITH [#3] – Ward 2, Cincinnati. 1830.

John SMITH [#4] - Ward 3, Cincinnati. 1830.

John SMITH [#1] – Ward 1, Cincinnati. 1840.

John SMITH [#2] – Ward 4, Cincinnati. 1840.

John SMITH [#3] – Ward 4, Cincinnati. 1840.

John SMITH [#4] – Ward 4, Cincinnati. 1840.

John SMITH [#5] – Ward 4, Cincinnati. 1840.

John SMITH [#6] – Ward 6, Cincinnati. 1840.

John SMITH – He worked as a butcher. He worked &/or lived on John Street between Kemble and Richmond. 1819.
John SMITH – He was a butcher. He worked &/or lived on Race above New Market. His nativity was Delaware. 1825.
John SMITH – He was a butcher. He worked &/or lived at the corner of Race and Wayne. 1829.

John SMITH – Worked as a cabinet maker working on Broadfoot. He lived on Seventh Street between Main & Walnut. 1819.
John B. SMITH – He was a cabinet maker. He worked &/or lived on Seventh between Main and Walnut. His nativity was England. 1825.

John SMITH – He was a cabinet maker at George Porter's. George is listed at Main between 6th and 7th. 1829.

John SMITH – He is a pork dealer. He worked &/or lived on Walnut between 5th and 6th. 1829.

John SMITH – There is a mention on 5 Feb 1830 in the Cincinnati Daily Gazette.

John SMITH – He was a pork merchant and worked at the corner of 10th and Walnut. Home was the corner of Walnut and 6th. 1831.
John SMITH. He was a pork merchant and had a business called John Smith & Co. at the southwest corner of Walnut and Court. Home: Northwest corner of Vine and 8th. 1836.

John SMITH – Worked as a gardener. He worked &/or lived at the north end of Race. 1819.

John SMITH – He was a merchant with a store at 29 Main. He lived on Sixth between Walnut and Vine. His nativity was Massachusetts. 1925.

John SMITH – He was a laborer. He boarded at Wm. Bird's. There is no listing for a Wm. Bird. 1829.

John SMITH - He was a river trader. He boarded at Mrs. Boggs'. This was a widow, Sarah Ann who had a boarding house on 'L. Market'. 1829.

John SMITH – He was a shoemaker. He worked &/or lived on 4th between Plumb and Western Row. 1829.
John SMITH – He was a shoe maker. He worked &/or lived on 6th between Plumb and Western Row. 1834.

John SMITH – He was a shoe maker. He worked &/or lived on Gano between Main and Walnut. 1834.

John SMITH – He was a tailor. He boarded at Mrs. Tomlinson's. This was Clara who had a boarding house on Sycamore near 4th. 1829.

John SMITH – This says only 'at J.W. Langdon's'. This is John W. who is shown at 'alley between 8th and 9th'. 1829.

John SMITH – He was a grocer. He worked &/or lived on 6th between Plumb and Western Row. 1831.

John SMITH – He was a grocer. He lived &/or worked 'S s New between Sycamore and Broadway.' 1836.

John SMITH – He was a stone cutter. He worked &/or lived at the rear of Elm between 3d and 4th. 1831.
John SMITH – He was a stone cutter. He worked &/or lived on 3d between Smith and Mill. 1834.
John SMITH – Stone mason. Home in Post-Office Alley. Nativity: Pennsylvania. 1840.

John SMITH – He was a writing-master. He worked &/or lived on 5th between Race and Elm. 1831.

John SMITH – He was a carpenter and boarded at Elizabeth Pearson's boarding house on Church alley. 1831.

John SMITH – He was a ship carpenter. He lived &/or worked on east Front near the corp. line. 1836.

John SMITH – No occupation listed. He boards at W. Lofthouse's. Lofthouse appears to be William who was a brewer and he worked &/or lived on 4th between John and Smith. 1831.

John SMITH – He was a soap maker. Stated is at William Christopher's. William also works at a soap factory and then stated is Northern liberties. 1831.

John SMITH – No occupation listed. Found on Walnut between 3d and 4th. 1834.

John SMITH – No occupation listed. He is found at the corner of New Market and Vine. 1834.

John SMITH – He was a stage driver. He worked &/or lived on Walnut between Front and 2d. 1834.

John SMITH – He was a stocking weaver. He boarded at John Lilley's who is shown as grocer. Lilly lived &/or worked at the northwest corner of 4th and Western Row. 1836.

John SMITH – He was a blacksmith at J. C. Norris' who was a blacksmith. The business was at west south Sycamore between 5th & 6th. 1836.

John SMITH – He was a blacksmith. He lived &/or worked on Water between Plum and Western Row. 1836.

John SMITH – He worked at or owned a business named Wm. SMITH & Sons, wine merchant. He lived &/or worked at 17 5th St. between Main and Walnut. 1836.

John SMITH - River Trader. Home: Front between Race and Elm. Nativity: Pennsylvania. 1840.

John SMITH – Cabinet maker at S Bartlett's [Bartlett & Roberts cabinet makers] located at 'S s Columbia St between Sycamore and Broadway. Boarded on Main north of Canal. Nativity: Switzerland. 1840.

John SMITH – Male, White, Single, age 62, death 4 Nov 1871 from heart disease. Home 366 Richmond. Sullivan undertaker. Burial Spring Grove. Nativity American.

John SMITH – Male, Colored, Married, age 62, death 8 Jan 1873 from inflammation of bladder. Home: 5th St. Nativity: Mo.

John SMITH – Male, White, Married, age 65 years, died 11 Jul 1879 from Diarrhea. He lived &/or died at 32 W. 6th St. Funeral director: J. Epply. Cemetery: Newport, KY. Occupation: Express. Nativity: Virginia.

John SMITH – Male, White, Married, age 59 died 17 Nov 1879 from hypertrophy of heart. He lived &/or died at E. 6th St. Funeral director: T. Mulvihill. Cemetery: St. Joseph's New. Occupation: Stone cutter. Nativity: England.

John B. SMITH – Ward 2, Cincinnati. 1820.

John B. SMITH John SMITH – Ward 5, Cincinnati. 1830.

John B. SMITH – No occupation listed. He worked &/or lived on 7th between Main and Walnut. 1831.

John D. SMITH – He was a printer. He worked &/or lived on Walnut between 6th and 7th. 1834.

John G. SMITH – Male, White, Married, age 69, died 6 Dec 1882 from Softening of Brain, He lived &/or died at 1505 Eastern Ave. Under taker: Watkins. Cemetery: Mt. Washington. Occupation: Weaver. Nativity: England.

John L. SMITH – Worked as a grocer. He worked &/or lived between Main and Walnut. His nativity was Massachusetts. 1825.

John L. SMITH – He was found on 7th between Race and Elm. 1836.

John M. SMITH – He was a stone cutter. He lived &/or worked on 3d between Smith and Mill. 1836.

John R. SMITH – He was a grocer. He worked &/or lived at the corner of Vine and Canal. 1829.
John R. SMITH – He was a grocer at John R. Smith & Scudder. The store he owned was at the corner of Vine and North Canal. 1831.
John R. SMITH - (Smith & Scudder) grocer. He worked &/or lived at the corner of Vine and Canal. 1834.

John W. SMITH – Salt Merchant at 9th between Main & Sycamore. Home: N s 7th between Main and Sycamore. Nativity: Ireland. 1840.
John W. SMITH – Ward 1, Cincinnati. 1840.

Jonas SMITH – He was an engine finisher. He lived &/or worked on Ludlow between Front and 2d. 1836.

Joseph SMITH – Ward 2, Cincinnati. 1820.

Joseph SMITH – Ward 3, Cincinnati. 1840.

Joseph SMITH – He was a laborer. He worked &/or lived on E. Front between Ludlow and Lawrence. His nativity was New Jersey. 1825.

Joseph SMITH – He was an innkeeper. He worked &/or lived Sixth between Plum and Western Row. His nativity was England. 1825.

Joseph SMITH – Cincinnati Insurance Company, Director. Office was at 22 Main Street. 1829.

Joseph SMITH – Ward 4, Cincinnati. 1830.

Joseph SMITH – He was an officer of The Cincinnati Savings Institution. This bank was incorporated in the winter of 1831 and was organized in March 1831. Its office for business is at "Goodman's Exchange Office," West Third Street. 1831.

Joseph SMITH – He was a director of the Cincinnati Savings Institution at No. 5 West Third Street. "Office open for receiving deposits on Mondays from 10 o'clock A.M. until 1 P.M."

Joseph SMITH – He was a director of the Commercial Bank on the east side of Main between Third and Fourth.

Jos. K. SMITH – Male, White, Widow. Age 83 years death 18 Feb 1874 from 'old age'. Lived or died on Ohio Ave. Occupation: Treasurer Insurance Co. Funeral director: J. Wiltsee. Burial Spring Grove. Nativity: Virginia.

Joseph SMITH – He was a carpenter. Then it says only 'New' which may be the street name. 1829.

Joseph SMITH – He was a stonecutter. He worked &/or lived on 3d between Vine and Race. 1831.

Joseph SMITH – He was a produce merchant on Canal between Main and Walnut. Home: 5th between Broadway and Pike. 1834.

Joseph SMITH – Produce Merchant on Sycamore near Canal Basin between 8th and 9th. Home: S s 4th between Broadway and Ludlow. Nativity: Virginia. 1840.

Joseph SMITH – He was a pork and produce merchant on Sycamore near canal. Home: '4th east Broadway'. 1836.

Joseph SMITH - Clerk at Graff's an auction and commission Merchant located at the corner of Main and Patterson's Alley. He boarded at the corner of 5th and Sycamore. Nativity: Pennsylvania. 1840.

Joseph C. SMITH – Ward 4, Cincinnati. 1840.

Joseph K. SMITH – He was a commission merchant with a store at 5 Lower Market. He lived on Third between main and Walnut. His nativity was Virginia. 1825.

Joseph K. SMITH - He worked &/or lived on 2d between Sycamore and Broadway. 1831.

Joshua SMITH – He was a house carpenter. He boarded at S. Pearson's. Samuel Pearson was also a carpenter and stated is that he lives or works on Race near Northern Row. 1831.

Josiah SMITH – He was a grocer. He worked &/or lived on Richmond between John and Western Row. 1819.

Josiah SMITH – Ward 2, Cincinnati. 1820.

Julius H. SMITH – He worked at or owned a grocery and liquor store. He lived &/or worked on 'W s Main between 9th and Court'. 1836.

Justus SMITH – Worked as a merchant. He worked &/or lived at 93 E. Front. 1819.

K First Names

Kosciouzko SMITH – He is a brass founder. He worked &/or lived at 85 Main. His nativity was Kentucky. 1825.

L First Names

L. B. Mrs. SMITH – She was a milliner. She lived &/or worked on 4th near Elm. 1836.

L. B. SMITH – Ward 5, Cincinnati. 1840.

Lemuel SMITH – He was a shoe maker. He worked &/or lived on High east of Canal. 1834.

Lewis SMITH – He was a brick maker. Then it only says 'London'. 1829.

Lewis SMITH – He was a butcher. He worked &/or lived at the corner of 9th and Race. 1829.

Lewis SMITH – He was a stonemason. He boards at Samuel Kissinger's who is also a stone mason. His home is on Water, near Walnut. 1829.

Lindsey SMITH – (col'd). He was a fireman on the river. He lived &/or worked on Cherry between Elm and Plum. 1836.

Lindsay SMITH – Ward 4, Cincinnati. 1840.

Lockey Mrs. SMITH – Milliner. She worked &/or lived at N s 6th between Elm & Plum. Nativity: N.J. 1840.

Lucinda SMITH – Female, White, Married, age 80 years died 5 Mar 1887 from 'Old Age – Congestion Lungs'. She lived &/or died at Sloo Alley. Under taker: Finn. Cemetery: Wesleyan. Nativity: U.S.

Lydia SMITH – Born 1759. Died unknown. Nativity: CT.

Lydia SMITH – Born 1788. Died 1845. Nativity: Ohio.

Lysabeth SMITH – Ward 6, Cincinnati. 1840.

M First Names

M. A. SMITH – Female, White, Widow, age 66 years, Died 12 Apr 1876 from Injury from fall debility.

Marcus SMITH – He is shown at the corner of Longworth and Smith which appears to be where he lived. No profession stated. 1819. She lived &/or died at 62 5th St. Funeral director: J. Wiltsee. Cemetery: Spring Grove. Nativity: France.

Marcus SMITH – He was a merchant. He worked &/or lived "Main front of the two steeple church." His nativity was Vermont. 1825.
Marcus SMITH – Home was on Race between 4th and 5th. 1829.
Marcus SMITH – Ward 2, Cincinnati. 1830.
Marcus SMITH – He was a merchant on Main. Home: Race between 4th and 5th. 1831.
Marcus SMITH (M. & S.S. SMITH) He worked at or owned a liquor store at the corner of Main and Court. Home: Race between 4th and 5th. 1834.
Marcus SMITH – He worked at or owned a liquor store. He lived &/or worked on Race between 4th and 5th. 1836.
Marcus SMITH – Home: Ss 7th between Race and Elm. Nativity: Vermont. 1840.
Marcus SMITH – Ward 5, Cincinnati. 1840.

Margaret SMITH [#1] – Ward 1, Cincinnati. 1840.

Margaret SMITH [#2] – Ward 7, Cincinnati. 1840.

Margaret SMITH – Listed as a male, White, Widow, age 76 years, died 6 Apr 1886 from Pheumatism. He/She lived &/or died at 294 State Ave. Funeral director: Linnemann. Cemetery: St. Bernard. Nativity: German.

Margaret SMITH – Female, White, Widow, age 90 years, died 21 Jul 1885 from 'Old Age'. She lived &/or died at 92 Avery St. Funeral director: Sullivan. Cemetery: St Joseph's New. Nativity: Ireland.

Margues SMITH – Ward 2, Cincinnati. 1820.

Maria SMITH – She was a washer woman. She lived &/or worked on Church alley. 1836.

Maria Mrs. SMITH – Tailoress. Home: Long between Plum & Western Row. Nativity: Virginia. 1840.

Martha SMITH – Ward 4, Cincinnati. 1840.

Martha A. SMITH – Female, White, Married. Death 26 Dec 1873, age 53 [born ca 1823], Bronchitis. Lived on Auburn Ave., Dr. Graham, Epply funeral director, burial Spring Grove.

Martin SMITH – He was a laborer. He worked &/or lived on 2d east of Mill. 1831.

Martin SMITH – He was a gardener. Shown is N. Liberties. 1834.

Mary SMITH [#1] – Ward 3, Cincinnati. 1830.

Mary SMITH [#2] – Ward 5, Cincinnati. 1830.

Mary SMITH [#1] – Ward 1, Cincinnati. 1840.

Mary SMITH [#2] – Ward 2, Cincinnati. 1840.

Mary SMITH [#3] – Ward 4, Cincinnati. 1840.

Mary SMITH [#4] – Ward 4, Cincinnati. 1840.

Mary SMITH [#5] – Ward 5, Cincinnati. 1840.

Mary SMITH [#6] – Ward 7, Cincinnati. 1840.

Mary / Polly SMITH – Born 1770. Died 1825. Nativity: PA.

Mary Mrs. SMITH – She was a weaver. She worked &/or lived on Richmond near John. 1831.
Mary SMITH – She was a carpet weaver. She lived &/or worked on Mercer between Walnut and Vine. 1836.

Mary Mrs. SMITH – Listed at Russell's alley between 4th & 5th. 1834.

Mary Mrs. SMITH – She is found on Court between Race and Elm. 1834.

Mary Mrs. SMITH – She was found listed at 'S s 5th between Sycamore and Broadway. 1836.
Mary Mrs. SMITH – Home: S s 5th between Sycamore and Broadway. Nativity: Connecticut. 1840.

Mary SMITH – Female, White, Widow, age 68, died 16 Jan 1883 from Phthisis Pulm. She lived &/or died at 8 State St. Funeral director: Mulvihill. Cemetery: St. Joseph's New. Nativity: Ireland.

Mary SMITH – Female, N, Married, age 66 died 11 Nov 1883 from Encephaloid tumor of Pelvis. She lived &/or died at 158 Van Horne St. Funeral director: Porter. Cemetery: Union Baptist. Nativity: Virginia.

Mary Ann SMITH – Female, White, Widowed, age 63, died 22 Feb 1882 from unknown cause. She lived &/or died at 6th & Elm St. Funeral director: Habig. Cemetery: Wesleyan. Occupation: Unknown. Nativity: Pennsylvania.

Mary H. SMITH – Ward 5, Cincinnati. 1840.

Mary L. SMITH – Female, White, Widow, age 83 years, died 30 Jan 1884 from paralysis. She lived &/or died at Mt. Lookout. Funeral director: Watkins. Cemetery: Spring Grove. Nativity: N.J.

Melinda SMITH – Ward 1, Cincinnati. 1840.

Merrick SMITH – He was a grocer. He worked &/or lived at the corner of 2d and Race. 1829.

Michael SMITH – He was a laborer. He worked &/or lived on Elm between Water and the river. 1831.

Mille SMITH — The profession was shoe binder. He/She worked &/or lived on Longworth between Western Row and John. Nativity was New York. 1825.

Mirick SMITH — He was a grocer. He worked &/or lived at the corner of Race and 2d. 1831.

Mordecai W. SMITH — He worked as a butcher. He worked &/or lived on Broadway between Eighth and Wayne. 1819.
Mordecai SMITH — He was a butcher. He worked &/or lived on Broadway near Seventh. His nativity was Virginia. 1825.
Mordecai SMITH — He was a grocer. He worked &/or lived at the corner of 2d and Race. (See Merrick.) 1829.
Mordecai SMITH — He was a butcher. He boarded at David Woodruff's on 10th near Deer Creek. 1831

Moses R. SMITH — He was a laborer. He boarded at G. H. SMITH's. This would be Green H. Smith. 1829.
Moses R. SMITH — He was an engineer and boarded at G. H. SMITH's. 1831.
Moses SMITH — He was an engineer. He worked &/or lived on Plumb near Front. 1834.
Moses R. SMITH — Engineer. Home: In Cherry Alley. Nativity: Kentucky. 1840.

Moses SMITH — Male, N, Widower, age 98 years, died Nov 1, 1887 from Bronchitis. He lived &/or died at 76 Chestnut St. Funeral director: Pirter. Stated is 'Colored American'. Nativity: Virginia.

N First Names

Nancy SMITH – Female, White, Married, age 81 died 14 Jun 1876 from Cirrhosis of Liver – Jaundice. She lived &/or died at 483 W. 7th St. Funeral director: J. Epply. Cemetery: Spring Grove. Nativity: N. Y.

Nathan SMITH – Birth 1765. Death 1839. Fought in the American Revolution. Nativity: New Jersey.

Nathan SMITH – He was a drayman. He worked &/or lived on 7th between John and Smith. 1834.

Nathan SMITH – He was a carpenter. He worked &/or lived on George between Western Row and John. 1834.

Nathan SMITH – He was a stone mason. He lived &/or worked on Western Row between 4th and 5th. 1836.

Nathaniel SMITH – He was a ship carpenter and then it says, 'Eastern liberties'. 1831.
Nathaniel SMITH – He was a carpenter. He worked &/or lived on 13th between Main and Walnut. 1834.
Nathaniel SMITH – Home: At S Crowell's. Nativity: Connecticut. 1840.

Nathan SMITH [#1] – Ward 7, Cincinnati. 1840.

Nathan SMITH [#2] – Ward 7, Cincinnati. 1840.

Nehemiah W. SMITH - Blacksmith at Williams & Miller's. Nativity: N.Y. 1840.

Nicholas SMITH – He worked at or owned a coffee house. He worked &/or lived on the corner of Canal and Elm. 1834.

Nicholas SMITH – Ward 1, Cincinnati. 1840.

O First Names

O. E. Mrs. SMITH – She was found on Front near Deer Creek bridge. (See Oliver Smith.) 1836.

Oliver SMITH – Worked as a merchant at 1 W. Fifth. Home: Sixth between Main & Sycamore. 1819
Oliver SMITH – Ward 2, Cincinnati. 1820.
Oliver SMITH – He was a merchant. He worked &/or lived on Broadway near Seventh. His nativity was Virginia. 1825.

Oliver SMITH - – Ward 3, Cincinnati. 1830.

Oliver SMITH – He was a salesman at Westcott's. He boarded at James Swafford's who lived on Longworth between vine and Race. 1836.
Oliver SMITH - Clerk at Westcott's located at No 24 5th street. This may have been a wholesale & retail boot and shoe store. Home: Longworth between Elm and Plum. Nativity: N.J. 1840.

Oliver SMITH – He was a cooper. He worked &/or lived on Front east of Deer Creek. (See O.E. Mrs. Smith.) 1829.

Oliver SMITH – No occupation listed. He boarded at A. W. Corey's. Corey was a bookseller and publisher with a business called Corey & Webster. He lived &/or worked on Vine between 9th and Court. 1836.

Oliver SMITH – Ward 5, Cincinnati. 1840.

P First Names

Patrick SMITH – Justice of the Peace for Whitewater Township, Hamilton Co., Ohio. 1819.

Patrick SMITH – County Officer, Associate Judge. 1829.

Patrick SMITH – Ward 6, Cincinnati. 1840.

Patrick SMITH – Male, White, Married, age 73, died 28 Jun 1880 from paralysis of Heart. He lived &/or worked at 78 Park St. The doctor was A. Carrick, Coroner. Under taker: Sullivan. Cemetery: St. Joseph's New. Occupation: Hack driver. Nativity: Ireland.

Peter SMITH – Born 1753. Died 1816. Nativity: NJ.

Peter SMITH – There is a Peter on the 1810 Hamilton County tax list.

Peter SMITH – Birth 1753. Death 1816. He fought in the American Revolution. Nativity: New Jersey.

Peter SMITH – Ward 2, Cincinnati. 1830.

Peter SMITH [#1] – Ward 2, Cincinnati. 1840.

Peter SMITH [#2] – Ward 4, Cincinnati. 1840.

Peter SMITH [#3] – Ward 7, Cincinnati. 1840.

Peter SMITH – He was a merchant near the corner of 5th and Walnut. Home: Near the corner of 4th and Plumb. 1831.

Peter SMITH – He works at 'fancy store' on 5th between Walnut and Vine. Home: 6th between Walnut and Vine. 1834.

Peter SMITH – He worked at or owned a fancy store on 5th between Walnut and Vine. Home: 6th between Walnut and Vine. 1836.

Peter SMITH – Worked at or owned a Comb, Jewelry and Fancy Store on 5th 1 door East of Walnut. Nativity: Maryland. 1840.

Peter SMITH – He was a river trader. He worked &/or lived on Front between Plumb and Elm. 1831.

Peter SMITH – He was a river trader. He lived &/or worked on Water between Elm and Plum. 1836.

Peter SMITH - River Trader. Home: Water between Elm and Plum. Nativity: Ireland. 1840.

Peter W. SMITH – No occupation listed. He was found at the corner of John and 6th. 1834.

Peter P. SMITH – Male, White, Married died 8 March 1868, age 83 years from 'old age'. Lived or died at 733 Everet. Worked as a laborer. Nativity: Germany.

Phebe SMITH – She is found at the corner of Ludlow and 3d. 1834.

Philip D. SMITH – Birth 1759. Death 1837. He fought in the American Revolution. Nativity: Maryland.

Phillip SMITH – He worked as a laborer. He worked &/or lived on Front near Steam-mill. 1831.

Philip SMITH – He was a grocer. He worked &/or lived on Sycamore between 2d and Lower Market. 1834.

Philip SMITH – He worked at or owned a boarding and coffee house on Sycamore between 2d and Lower Market. 1836.

Philip SMITH – Cooper. He boarded on Front between Vine and Race. Nativity: Maryland. 1840.

Pleasant Mrs. SMITH – Washer woman. Home: Front between Vine and Race. Nativity: Kentucky. 1840.
Pleasant SMITH – Ward 4, Cincinnati. 1840.

Pulaski SMITH – He was a druggist. He worked &/or lived on Main between 10th and Canal. 1831.
Pulaski SMITH – He was a druggist at the corner of Court and Main. Home: 13th between Vine and Race. 1834.
Pulaski SMITH – He was a druggist at the 'W s Main' between Court and Canal. He boarded at the Main St. Hotel. 1836.

R First Names

R. C. SMITH – No occupation listed. He boarded at the Pearl St. House. 1836.

R. Sheaff SMITH - Druggist at Lewis Stagg's at the corner Walnut & 6th. Nativity: Pennsylvania. 1840.

Ralph P. SMITH – He was a merchant. He worked &/or lived at 20 Main. His nativity was New Jersey. 1825.

Rebecca SMITH – Ward 2, Cincinnati. 1830.

Rebecca Mrs. SMITH – She is shown at Longworth between Western Row and John. 1829.
Rebecca SMITH – She is shown on Western Row between 5th and Longworth. 1831.
Rebecca Mrs. SMITH – She is found at the corner of Plumb and 6th. 1834.
Rebecca Mrs. SMITH - Seamstress. Home: Water between Vine and Race. Nativity: Ireland. 1840.

Rhoda Allison SMITH – Born 1801. Died 1840. Nativity: Ohio.

Richard H. SMITH – He was a carpenter. Then it says, 'At Jas. Smith's, New' which New is most likely the street name. 1829.

Robert SMITH [#1] – Ward 1, Cincinnati. 1820.

Robert SMITH [#2] – Ward 1, Cincinnati. 1820.

Robert SMITH [#3] – Ward 3, Cincinnati. 1820.

Robert SMITH [#1] – Ward 1, Cincinnati. 1830.

Robert SMITH [#2] – Ward 5, Cincinnati. 1830.

Robert SMITH – Ward 6, Cincinnati. 1840.

Robert SMITH – Worked as a house carpenter. He worked &/or lived on Broadway between Seventh & Eighth. 1819.
Robert SMITH – He was a carpenter. He worked &/or lived on Broadway between New and Seventh. His nativity was Maryland. 1825.
Robert SMITH – He was a carpenter. He worked &/or lived on Broadway between 7th and New. 1829.
Robert SMITH – He was a carpenter. He worked &/or lived on Broadway between 6th & 7th. 1831.
Robert SMITH – He was a carpenter. He worked &/or lived on Alley between 4th & 5th. 1834.

Robert SMITH – He was a carpenter. He lived &/or worked on Long between John and Western Row. 1836.
Robert SMITH - Carpenter. Home: N s Long between Smith and Mound. Nativity: Virginia. 1840.

Robert SMITH – He is an agent for Norris & Egerton, 'Front near Lud.' 1829.

Robert SMITH – He was a mill-stone maker. He worked &/or lived on Front near Ludlow. 1831.
Robert SMITH – He was a mill stone maker. He worked &/or lived on 7th between Sycamore and Broadway. 1834.

Robert SMITH – He was a barber. He worked on South Canal between Race and Vine. Home: Main between Canal and 12th. 1831.

Robert SMITH – He was a clerk at Corey & Fairbank bookseller and publisher on Main near the corner of 5th. 1834.

Robert SMITH – He was a saddler. He boarded at Mrs. Ann Tucker's boarding house at 'N s 5th between Vine and Race'. 1836.

Ross SMITH – Ward 3, Cincinnati. 1830.

Ruth SMITH – Born 1801. Death 1854. Nativity: Ohio.

S First Names

S. SMITH S. W. SMITH – Ward 4, Cincinnati. 1830.

S. P. SMITH - [West & Smith] Boarded on Sycamore between 4lh and 5th. Nativity: Ohio. 1840.

S. S. SMITH - Produce, Grocery and Liquor Dealer, N s W Front between Main and Walnut. Home: S s 4th between Race and Elm. Nativity: N.Y. 1840.

S. S. SMITH – Ward 1, Cincinnati. 1830.

S. S. SMITH – Male, White, Married, age 82, died May 4 1885 from fracture of femur. He lived &/or died at 7 Mt. Auburn Ave. Funeral home: Wiltsee. Cemetery: Spring Grove. Occupation: Retired. Nativity: N.Y.

S. W. SMITH - Produce Merchant. Corner of west W Front & Walnut. 1840.

S. W. SMITH – Carpenter. Home: N s Geo between Western Row and John. Nativity: Maine. 1840.

Sally SMITH – Ward 4, Cincinnati. 1830.

Sally SMITH – (col'd) She was a washer woman. She lived &/or worked on Vine between Race and Elm. 1836.

Samuel SMITH – There is a Samuel on the 1810 Hamilton County tax list.

Samuel SMITH – Worked as a laborer. Home &/or work is 286 Main. 1819.

Samuel SMITH – Ward 3, Cincinnati. 1820.

Samuel SMITH – He was a sawyer. He worked &/or lived at 'alley' between Lawrence and Pike. His nativity was Virginia. 1825.

Samuel SMITH [#1] – Ward 1, Cincinnati. 1830.

Samuel SMITH [#2] – Ward 2, Cincinnati. 1830.

Samuel SMITH [#3] – Ward 3, Cincinnati. 1830.

Samuel SMITH [#4] – Ward 5, Cincinnati. 1830.

Samuel SMITH – He was a cooper and worked on Fifth. He lived on Walnut between Fifth and Sixth streets. His nativity was Virginia. 1825.
Samuel SMITH – He was a cooper. He worked &/or lived on Walnut between 4th and 5th. 1829.
Samuel SMITH – He was a cooper. He worked &/or lived on George between Western Row and John. 1834.
Samuel SMITH - Cooper. Home: Long between Plum and Western Row. Nativity: Virginia. 1840.

Samuel SMITH – He worked as a butcher. He worked &/or lived at the corner of Race and 12th. 1831.
Saml. SMITH – He was a butcher. He worked &/or lived on 12th between Race and Elm. 1834.

Samuel SMITH - Butcher. Home: 'Jno between Elizabeth & Chesnut.' Nativity: Maryland. 1840.

Samuel SMITH – Butcher. Home: S s Court between Plum & Western Row. 1840.

Samuel SMITH – He worked as a pork merchant. Then listed is only 'Friendship'. 1831.

Samuel SMITH – He was a pork dealer. He worked &/or lived on Elizabeth between Western Row and John. 1834.

Samuel SMITH – He was a pork cutter. He lived &/or worked on Elizabeth between Western Row and John. 1836.

Samuel SMITH – He was a shoe maker. He lived &/or worked on High near the corp. line. 1836.

Samuel SMITH – He was a shoe maker. He boarded at James Eshelby's. Eshelby was a shoemaker who lived &/or worked at 'N s 5th between Vine and Race'. 1836.

Samuel SMITH – Shoe maker. Home: E Front east of Rolling Mill. Nativity: Pennsylvania. 1840.

Samuel SMITH [#1] – Ward 1, Cincinnati. 1840.

Samuel SMITH [#2] – Ward 2, Cincinnati. 1840.

Samuel SMITH [#3] – Ward 5, Cincinnati. 1840.

Samuel SMITH [#4] – Ward 5, Cincinnati. 1840.

Samuel P. SMITH – No occupation listed. He is found at Christopher Smith's. 1836.

Samuel R. SMITH – Ward 2, Cincinnati. 1840.

Samuel S. SMITH – He was a merchant. He worked &/or lived at 173 Main. His nativity was New York. 1825.

Samuel S. SMITH – He was a grocer. He worked &/or lived at the corner of 9th and Main. 1829.

Samuel S. SMITH – He worked at or owned a liquor store. He worked &/or lived at the corner of 9th and Main. 1831.

Samuel S. SMITH – He is a merchant. He lived &/or worked on 7th between Walnut and Vine. 1836.

Samuel S. SMITH – Ward 2, Cincinnati. 1840.

Samuel T. SMITH – No occupation listed. He worked &/or lived on Charles between Elm and Plumb. 1834.

Samuel T. SMITH – He works at or owns T. & Co., a grocery at the southwest corner of Vine and Canal. Home: Race near Canal. 1836.

Samuel T. SMITH – '[S. T. & S.S.]' Home: Northwest corner 6th & Plum. Nativity: N.Y. 1840.

S. W. SMITH – Ward 5, Cincinnati. 1830.

S. W. [Samuel W.] SMITH – He was a carpenter. He is listed on George between Western Row and John. (See Sarah Mrs.) 1829.

Samuel W. SMITH – He was a carpenter. He worked &/or lived on George near Western Row. 1831.

Samuel W. SMITH – He was a carpenter. He worked &/or lived on George between Western Row and John. 1834.

Samuel W. SMITH – He was a carpenter. He lived &/or worked on George near John. 1836.

Samuel W. SMITH – Ward 7, Cincinnati. 1840.

Sarah SMITH – She was a widow and is shown on Race between Front and 2d. 1831.

Sarah SMITH [#1] – Ward 4, Cincinnati. 1840.

Sarah SMITH [#2] – Ward 7, Cincinnati. 1840.

Sarah SMITH [#3] – Ward 7, Cincinnati. 1840.

Sarah SMITH [Mrs.] – Female, White, Married, age 67, died 14 Aug 1880 from Mitral Insufficiency. She lived &/or died on Livingston St. Under taker: Epply. Cemetery: Spring Grove. Nativity: N.J.

Sarah Mrs. SMITH – She is listed on George between Western Row and John. 1829. This may be the same person as below. (See S.W. SMITH.) 1829.

Sarah Mrs. SMITH – She is listed on Front between Elm and Plumb. 1829. This may be the same person as above with a move. 1829.

Sarah Mrs. SMITH – Home: Pike between 3d and Congress. Nativity: Ohio. 1840.

Sarah M. SMITH – Death 2 Nov 1866, age 69 [born ca 1797], Cholera. Nativity: Pennsylvania. Female, White, Widowed. Home: 182 Water St.

Siney [Sidney] SMITH – He was a harness maker and trimmer. He worked &/or lived on Sycamore between Third and Fourth. His nativity was D.C. (District of Columbia). 1825.

Sidney SMITH – He was a coach trimmer and boarded at the John Elstner [Elster] boarding house at the corner of Broadway and 6th. 1834.

Silas SMITH – He worked as a grocer at 3 W. Fifth. He lives on Longworth between John and Smith. 1819.
Silas SMITH – Ward 2, Cincinnati. 1820.
Silas SMITH (Silas Smith & Co.) Owner of a wholesale grocery on Main near Canal. Home: Court between Main and Walnut. 1834.
Silas SMITH – He worked at or owned a wholesale grocery at 'E s Main' near Canal. Home: Court between Elm and Plum. 1836.

Silas SMITH - Coach maker. He boarded at E Poor's. Nativity: N.Y. 1840.

Silas SMITH – Ward 5, Cincinnati. 1840.

Silas SMITH - [Smith & McMillen] Home: N s Court between Elm & Plum. Nativity: Vermont. 1840.

Simon SMITH – No employment listed. He lives at the corner of Walnut and Water. His nativity is Pennsylvania. 1825.

Solomon F. SMITH – Ward 1, Cincinnati. 1830.

Sophia Mrs. SMITH – She is listed on John between 9th and Richmond. 1829.

Sophia Mrs. SMITH – She worked as a seamstress. She worked &/or lived on Western Row between 7th and London. 1831.

Sophia SMITH – She was a widow. She is shown on 5th between Western Row and John. 1831.

Sophia SMITH – She is a widow. She is found on London west of Fulton. 1834.

Spencer SMITH – Male, White, Married, age 59 died on 4 Oct 1879 from Consumption. He lived &/or died at 585 E. 3rd St. Funeral director: Estep & Meyer. Cemetery: Spring Grove. He was a carpenter. Nativity: U.S.

Stafford B. SMITH - Machinist. Home: E s John between 4th and 5th. Nativity: Massachusetts. 1840.
Stafford B. SMITH – Ward 6, Cincinnati. 1840.

Steven SMITH – Ward 5, Cincinnati. 1830.

Susan SMITH – She was a washer. She worked &/or lived at Seventh between Plum and Western Row. Her nativity was Maryland. 1825.

Susan SMITH – Female, White, Married, age 72, died 26 Mar 1885 from Peritonitis. She lived &/or died on Highland Ave. Funeral director: Wiltsee. Cemetery: Spring Grove. Nativity: Ohio.

Susanna SMITH – Land owner 96.8 acres, dated 30 Sep 1825.

Sylvester SMITH – He was a drayman. He lived &/or worked on Canal between elm and Plum. 1836.

Sylvester SMITH - [S. T. & S. S.] Home: 'Lond between Carr & Frmn.' Nativity: N.Y. 1840.

T First Names

Theodore SMITH – He was a carpenter. He worked &/or lived Theodore SMITH - Carpenter at T. Williamson's. Home: Western Row between George and 6th. Nativity: Maryland. 1840. on 4th between Elm and Plumb. 1834.
Theodore SMITH - Carpenter at T. Williamson's. Home: Western Row between George and 6th. Nativity: Maryland. 1840.

Theophilus SMITH – Ward 7, Cincinnati. 1840.

Thomas SMITH – Born 1719.

Thomas Edward SMITH – Born 1783. Died 1841. Nativity: Virginia.

Thomas SMITH [#1] – Ward 2, Cincinnati. 1820.

Thomas SMITH [#2] – Ward 3, Cincinnati. 1820.

Thomas SMITH – Worked as a block & pump maker. He worked &/or lived at 75 E. Front. 1819.
Thomas SMITH – He was a block and pump maker. He worked &/or lived at E. Front between Ludlow and Lawrence. His nativity was New York. 1825.
Thomas SMITH – He worked as a pump maker on E. Front. Home: Water near Elm. 1829.
Thos. SMITH – He was a block and pump maker. He worked &/or lived on Water between Elm and Plumb. 1834.

Thomas SMITH – He was a grocer. He worked &/or lived on Water between Plumb and Elm. 1831.

Thomas SMITH – He was a grocer and is found at 'E. Liberties'. 1834.

Thomas SMITH – He was a grocer. He lived &/or worked on Water between Elm and Plum. 1836.

Thomas SMITH – He is shown on Front west of Western Row. 1829.

Thomas SMITH [#1] – Ward 3, Cincinnati. 1830.

Thomas SMITH [#2] – Ward 4, Cincinnati. 1830.

Thomas SMITH [#3] – Ward 4, Cincinnati. 1830.

Thomas SMITH [#4] – Ward 5, Cincinnati. 1830.

Thomas SMITH [#1] – Ward 1, Cincinnati. 1840.

Thomas SMITH [#2] – Ward 5, Cincinnati. 1840.

Thomas SMITH – He was a comb maker. He worked &/or lived at 221 Main. His nativity was Maryland. 1825.

Thomas SMITH – Worked as a cabinetmaker. He worked &/or lived at 239 Main. 1819.

Thomas SMITH – He was a cabinet maker. He worked &/or lived at 239 Main. His nativity is England. 1825.

Thomas SMITH – He was a fisherman. He boards at Mrs. Sarah Pettit's on Front near Wood. 1829.

Thomas SMITH – He was a fisherman. He worked &/or lived on Front below 5th. 1834.

Thomas SMITH – He was a fisherman. He lived &/or worked at the junction of Front and 5th. 1836.

Thomas SMITH – No occupation listed. He worked &/or lived on Elm between 9th and 10th. 1831.

Thomas SMITH – it says "[Ross & Smith] Walnut between 6th and 7th." 1831.

Thomas SMITH – All that is stated is 'East Front'. 1831.

Thomas SMITH – He was a laborer. He worked &/or lived on Front between Butler and Bridge. 1834.

Thomas SMITH – Male, White, Married, age 60, death 20 Aug 1869 from Typhoid Fever. Lived or died at 390 Race. Eppley funeral director. Burial Spring Grove.

Thomas SMITH - Mill Stone maker. Home: Water between Plum and Western Row. Nativity: N.C. 1840.

Thomas SMITH – Male, White, Widower, age 67, died 12 Apr 1881 from Paralysis. He lived &/or died on Gilbert Ave. Funeral director: Estep. Cemetery: Spring Grove. Occupation: Shoe maker. Nativity: Ireland.

Thomas SMITH – Male, N, Widower, age 63 died from dropsy on 2 Oct 1883. He lived &/or died on Gilbert Ave. Funeral director: Habig. Occupation: Stable Boss. Nativity: Colored American.

Thomas B. SMITH - Trader. Home: S s 9th West of Walnut. Nativity: Massachusetts. 1840.

Thomas D. SMITH – Ward 2, Cincinnati. 1830.
Thomas D. SMITH – He was a drayman. He worked &/or lived on 4th. 1831.
Thomas D. SMITH – No occupation listed. Shown at Alley between Mill and Stone, south of 4th. 1834.

Thomas Edward SMITH – Born 1783. Died 1841. Nativity: Virginia.

Thomas F. SMITH – Male, White, Widower, age 88 years, died 31 Aug 1885 from Chr. Bronchitis. He lived &/or died at 400 Eastern Ave. Funeral director: Watkins. Cemetery: Spring Grove. Occupation: Grocer. Nativity: Pennsylvania.

Thomas J. SMITH – Ward 5, Cincinnati. 1830.
Thomas J. SMITH – He worked as a mason. He worked &/or lived on Western Row near Elizabeth. 1831.
Thos. J. SMITH – He was a stone mason. He boarded at W. Smiths. 1834.
Thomas J. SMITH – He was a stone mason. He boarded at Wm. Smith's at Western Row near Hospital. 1836.

Thomas P. SMITH – Ward 5, Cincinnati. 1830.

W First Names

W. B. SMITH – He owned or worked at Truman & Smith book sellers. He worked &/or lived 150 Main. 1834.

Walter SMITH – Ward 1. Cincinnati. 1820.

Washington SMITH – He was a carpenter. He boarded at Jacob Staley's who is shown on 19th between Main and Walnut. 1831.
Washington SMITH – He was a carpenter. He worked &/or lived on Clay between 12th and 13th. 1834.
Washington SMITH – He was a carpenter. He lived &/or worked on Clay near 12th. 1836.

Westley SMITH – He was a laborer. He boarded at John Henry's shown as 'N. Liberties'.

William SMITH – Birth 1760. Death 1841. He fought in the American Revolution. Nativity: Virginia.

William SMITH – Worked as a whitesmith at 40 S. Sycamore. Home: 37 Sycamore. 1819.

William SMITH [#1] – Ward 2, Cincinnati. 1820.

William SMITH [#2] – Ward 2, Cincinnati. 1820.

William SMITH [#3] – Ward 2, Cincinnati. 1820.

William SMITH [#4] – Ward 3, Cincinnati. 1820.

William SMITH [#1] - Ward 2, Cincinnati. 1830.

William SMITH [#2] - Ward 2, Cincinnati. 1830.

William SMITH [#3] – Ward 3, Cincinnati. 1830.

William SMITH [#4] – Ward 5, Cincinnati. 1830.

William SMITH – He was a shoemaker. He worked &/or lived on Longworth between Smith and Mound. His nativity was Ireland. 1825.

William SMITH – He was a shoemaker. He boards at John Crother's on Broadway between 7th and 8th. 1829.

William SMITH – He was a shoe maker. He worked &/or lived on 5th between Elm and Plumb. 1834.

William SMITH – He was a shoemaker. He boarded at Joel Perkin's. Perkins was a chair manufacturer and lived or worked on Plum between Plum and Western Row. 1836.

William SMITH – Shoe maker. He lived &/or worked at the Southeast corner of 5th and Broadway. Nativity: Virginia. 1840.

William SMITH – He was a laborer. He worked &/or lived on E. Front near the Steam Mill. His nativity was England. 1825.

William SMITH – He was a laborer. He worked &/or lived on Western Row between Elizabeth and Chestnut. 1834.

William SMITH – He was a laborer. He lived &/or worked on Western Row near Commercial Hospital. 1836.

William SMITH – He was a "tailor, Lower Market, shop E. Front between Broadway and Ludlow." His nativity was Ireland. 1825.

William SMITH – He was a tailor. He worked &/or lived on Water between Main and Walnut. 1829.

William SMITH – He was a tailor. He lived &/or worked on 'N s Water between Main and Walnut. 1836.

William SMITH - [Sanders & Smith] Home: Green between Race and Elm. Nativity: Virginia. 1840.

William SMITH – Male, White, Single died 12 Aug 1866 from 'old age'. He lived &/or died at 308 5th St. He was a tailor. Nativity: Ireland.

William SMITH – He was a blacksmith. He worked &/or lived on Front near Pike. 1829.
William SMITH – He worked as a blacksmith. He boarded at William Wyatt's, a shoemaker, near the corner of Congress and Lawr. 1831.

William SMITH – He is listed as having an iron store and is a commission merchant. He worked &/or lived on Front between Main and Walnut. 1831.

William SMITH – He was a wagon maker. He worked &/or lived on Race above Canal. 1829.

William SMITH – No occupation listed. He lived or worked on Western Row near Elizabeth. 1829.

William SMITH – Vice President, Scott's Benevolent Society. 1829.

William SMITH – Listed is 'saddler Grove'. It appears to mean he is working as a saddler on the street Grove. 1831

William SMITH – He was a drayman. He worked &/or lived on Gano between Vine and Walnut. 1831.

William SMITH – He was a drayman. He worked &/or lived on Front between Lawrence and Pike. 1834.

William SMITH – He was a drayman. He lived &/or worked on John between Catharine and Elizabeth. 1836.

William SMITH – He was a tailor and worked on Water near Walnut. Home was on Union alley.1831.

William SMITH – He was a tailor on 3d north of the Post Office. Home: corner of Green and Elm. 1834.

William SMITH – He was a merchant – tailor at 3d near Main. Home: Elm between 3d and 4th. 1836.

William SMITH – He was a physician. He worked &/or lived on Elm between 4th and 5th. 1831.

William SMITH – No occupation listed. Worked &/or lived on Front near Deer Creek bridge. 1831.

William SMITH – He was a teamster. He worked &/or lived on Farrar between Plumb and Western Row. 1834.

William SMITH – (col'd). He was a steward on the river. He lived &/or worked on Front between Vine and Race. 1836.

William SMITH Junior – He worked at and owned Wm. Smith & Sons, wine merchant at 17 West 5th st. 1836.

William SMITH, Dr. – He worked at or owned W. Smith & Sons and is listed as a wine merchant. He worked &/or lived on 5th between Main and Walnut. 1834.

William SMITH M.D. - Home: 3 miles North of Corporation line. 1840.

William SMITH - Laborer. Home: W s Western Row near Elizabeth. Nativity: N.Y. 1840.

William SMITH - Butcher. Home: Jackson between Canal and 12th. Nativity: Pennsylvania. 1840.

William SMITH [#1] – Ward 1, Cincinnati. 1840.

William SMITH [#2] – Ward 2, Cincinnati. 1840.

William SMITH [#3] – Ward 5, Cincinnati. 1840.

William SMITH [#4] – Ward 7, Cincinnati. 1840.

William SMITH [#5] – Ward 7, Cincinnati. 1840.

William SMITH & Sons – Wine merchants at 17 West 5th St. 1836.

William B. SMITH – Ward 2, Cincinnati. 1840.

William B. SMITH – He was a cabinet maker. He worked &/or lived at Chris Smith's. 1829.

William B. SMITH - Carpenter at Coolidge's which was on 3d opposite the post office. He boarded at Mrs. Peebles boarding house on S s 3rd almost opposite the post office. Nativity: N.Y. 1840.

William B. SMITH – He was a clerk. He worked &/or lived at R. Hurd's who was a dry goods merchant. Hurd is listed as working or living on Main between 4th & 5th. 1831.

William B. SMITH – No occupation listed. He boards at Christopher Smith's. 1836. He worked &/or lived on 4th between Main and Sycamore. 1836.

William C. SMITH - Paver. Home: John between 'Cath' & Elizabeth. Nativity: N.Y. 1840.

William H. SMITH – Male, Widower, age 68 years, died 28 Sep 1884 from Paralysis. He lived &/or died on Auburn Ave. Funeral director: Epply. Cemetery: Spring Grove. Occupation: Physician. Nativity: Cincinnati.

William J. SMITH - Shoe maker. Home: Broadway opposite Franklin. Nativity: N.Y. 1840.

William J. SMITH [#1] – Ward 1, Cincinnati. 1840.

William J. SMITH [#2] – Ward 1, Cincinnati. 1840.

William John SMITH – Sycamore Township. Age 16-26, wife age 16-26, son 1 age up to 10. Occupation: Agriculture. 1820.

William M. SMITH – He was a grocer. He worked &/or lived on Front between Elm and Plum. His nativity was Pennsylvania. 1825.
William M. SMITH – He was a grocer. He worked &/or lived on Front east of Deer creek. 1829.
William M. SMITH – Ward 3, Cincinnati. 1830.
William M. SMITH – He was a grocer. He worked &/or lived on East Front. 1831.
William SMITH – He was a grocer. He worked &/or lived on East Front near 'Cor. Line'. 1834.

William O. SMITH - Bar-keeper at Montgomery's on 6th. Nativity: N.J. 1840.

William R. SMITH – He worked at and maybe owned 'Wright Smith Senior & Co.' as a grocer. 1836.

William R. SMITH - Home: Head of Vine street. Nativity: Massachusetts. 1840.

William S. SMITH – He was a clerk. He worked &/or lived on 6th between John and Smith. 1829.

William S. SMITH – Secretary, Erin Benevolent Society. 1829.

William S. SMITH – Ward 4, Cincinnati. 1830.
William S. SMITH – He was a clerk at A.C. Brown's wholesale dry goods at 37 Main. 1831.

William S. SMITH – He was a produce merchant on Front between main and Walnut. Home: George between Race and Elm. 1834.

William S. SMITH – He was a grocer and distiller at 13 W. Front. Home: 6th between John and Smith. 1836.

William T. SMITH – Sycamore Township. Age 26-45, wife age 16-26, son 1 up to age 10. Occupation: Agriculture. 1820.

William SMITH – Male, White, Single, age 59 years. Death 14 Dec1878 from Dysentery. Funeral home director: H. Jones. Burial at City Cemetery. Nativity: U.S.

William SMITH – Male, White, Married, age 50 years. Died 11 Apr 1878 from 'Phthisis Pulm'. He lived &/or died on

New St. He was a marble polisher. Funeral director: Sullivan. Cemetery: St. Joseph's Old. Nativity: Ireland.

Willman SMITH – Male, White, Married, age 74 died 27 Dec 1870 from Pneumonia. He was a statesman. Funeral director: Habig. Burial: Madison. Nativity: Vermont.

William SMITH – Male, White, Widower, age 83 years, died 2 Oct 1883 due to Myocarditis. He lived &/or died at Plum & 9th St. Funeral director: Sullivan. Cemetery: St. Joseph's New. Occupation: Laborer. Nativity: Ireland.

Winthrop B. SMITH – He worked at &/or owned Truman & Smith bookseller.
Winthrop B. SMITH - [Truman & Smith] Home: E s Race between 4th & 5th. Nativity: Connecticut. 1840.

Wright SMITH – He worked as a distiller. He worked &/or lived at the corner of John and Richmond. 1819.

Wright SMITH – Ward 2, Cincinnati. 1820.

Wright SMITH – He was a merchant. He worked &/or lived at 2 Commercial Row. His nativity was Vermont. 1825.

Wright SMITH – Ward 2, Cincinnati. 1830.

Wright SMITH [#1] – Ward 2, Cincinnati. 1840.

Wright SMITH [#2] – Ward 5, Cincinnati. 1840.

Wright SMITH & Co. – Grocery and liquor store at 135 Main. 1836.

Wright SMITH & Co. – Wholesale grocers. Southeast corner of Main and Court. 1836.

Wright SMITH Sr - Merchant. Home: southeast corner of Race & 6th. Nativity: Vermont. 1840.

Wright SMITH – See businesses, wholesale grocer. He lived at the corner of 6th and Race. 1829.

Wright SMITH (W. Smith & Co.). He worked &/or lived at the corner of Race and 6th. 1831.

Wright SMITH Senior (Wright Smith & Co.) This is found at the southeast corner of 6th & Race. 1836.

Wright SMITH – He was a director of the Lafayette Bank. "The Franklin and Lafayette Banks are now erecting elegant and commodious Banking Houses on third street near the Post Office, which will be completed during the present season, after which the Banks will there be permanently located." 1836.

Wright SMITH Sen. [senior] – He was a director of the Cincinnati Savings Institution at No. 5 West Third Street. "Office open for receiving deposits on Mondays from 10 o'clock A.M. until 1 P.M." 1836.

Wright SMITH Jr & Co., Wholesale Grocers, No 145 Main. 1840.

Wright SMITH Jr - [W. SMITH & Co.] Home: S s 7th between Main & Walnut. Nativity: Massachusetts. 1840.

Wright SMITH – No occupation listed. He is found at the corner of Race and 6th. 1834.

Wright G. SMITH, Junior – No occupation listed. He boards at Wright Smith's. 1834.

Wright SMITH Junior – Worked and owner of Wright Smith & Co., wholesale grocer. He lived at Wm. M. Walker's.

Walker is shown as a merchant who lived &/or worked at 'E s Broadway between 3d and 4th'. 1836.

SMYTH Last Name

G. B. SMYTH & Co. [George B. Smyth & Lawrence McDonough] dry good merchants. He worked &/or lived at No. 31 Main near Front.

John SMYTH – He was a grocer. He worked &/or lived on New between Sycamore and Broadway. 1831.

John W. SMYTH – No occupation shown. He boarded at John L. Richmond's boarding house. Richmond was also a physician. He worked &/or lived at the corner of Walnut and Water. 1831.

William SMYTHE – He works at or owns a clothing store on Water between Main and Walnut. Home: George between Smith and Mound. 1834.

William SMYTH - Merchant Tailor, N s Water between Commercial Row & Walnut. Nativity: Ireland. 1840.

.

1802 Stonebridge Map

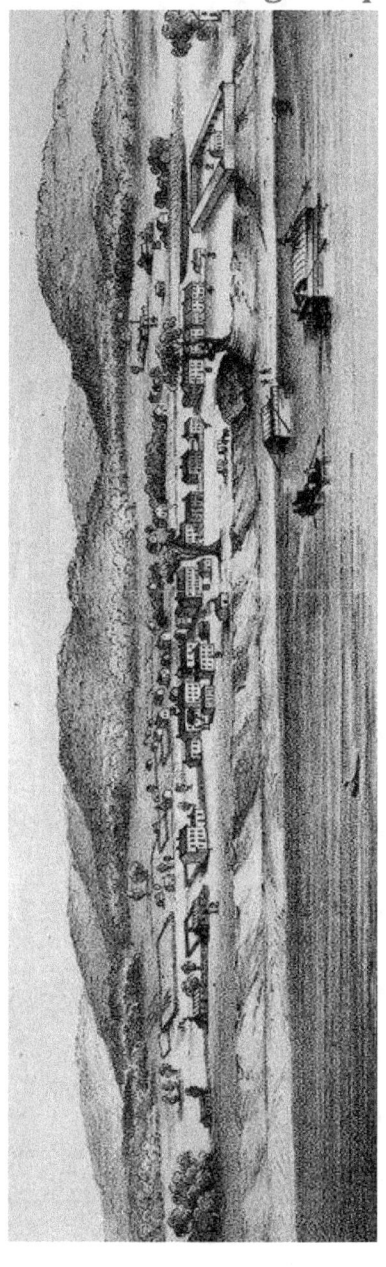

Sources

- Birth and Death records created by the Hamilton County Health Department, housed at the University of Cincinnati.
- Hamilton County, Cincinnati City Directories
- Deeds
- 1810 Tax List
- Daughters of the American Revolution
- The Church of Jesus Christ of Latter-Day Saints
- First families of Cincinnati index.